STEAM JOBS IN
GAME
DEVELOPMENT

Kenneth Rosenberg

Rourke
Educational Media

rourkeeducationalmedia.com

Scan for Related Titles and Teacher Resources

Before Reading:

Building Academic Vocabulary and Background Knowledge

Before reading a book, it is important to tap into what your child or students already know about the topic. This will help them develop their vocabulary, increase their reading comprehension, and make connections across the curriculum.

1. *Look at the cover of the book. What will this book be about?*
2. *What do you already know about the topic?*
3. *Let's study the Table of Contents. What will you learn about in the book's chapters?*
4. *What would you like to learn about this topic? Do you think you might learn about it from this book? Why or why not?*
5. *Use a reading journal to write about your knowledge of this topic. Record what you already know about the topic and what you hope to learn about the topic.*
6. *Read the book.*
7. *In your reading journal, record what you learned about the topic and your response to the book.*
8. *After reading the book complete the activities below.*

Content Area Vocabulary

Read the list. What do these words mean?

art assets
artificial intelligence
bugs
conversion rate
crunch
drop rates
exploit
feedback
mechanic
microtransactions
virtual economy

After Reading:

Comprehension and Extension Activity

After reading the book, work on the following questions with your child or students in order to check their level of reading comprehension and content mastery.

1. *Name several things a video game tester does.* (Summarize)
2. *Who is considered the core of a game development team?* (Infer)
3. *What is HTML?* (Asking questions)
4. *Who creates the visual elements of a video game?* (Text to self connection)
5. *What is a sound engineer's role in creating a video game?* (Asking questions)

Extension Activity

Video games are a favorite hobby for not just children but also adults. After reading the book, you can see how many people are involved and how much time it takes to create a new game. Do any of these jobs appeal to you? Pick just one and write down all the things they do, the important things you would need to study in order to obtain this job and what things you would do to contribute or make things even better! Be creative. You could be part of the future of video game production.

Table of Contents

What Is STEAM?

A game designer helps a development team create the story and rules for a new video game. A game programmer writes computer code to create a virtual environment. An audio engineer records and mixes sound effects and dialogue to make the game more realistic.

What do all these people have in common? It's not just video games! All of their jobs require a STEAM education.

What does STEAM stand for?

Science
Technology
Engineering
Art
Math

Some of the most exciting careers are in STEAM fields. A strong STEAM education will allow you to research, test, and build new things. The problem-solving skills learned through STEAM can take you to the next level in just about any career field.

Audio engineers record and edit music and sound effects.

Game programmers write code to build virtual characters and environments.

Game Design

Video games have images and sounds just like movies, but video games are different because they are also interactive. They require input from players who use a controller to tell the game what to do next.

Video games are entertaining because they challenge players by giving them fun abilities to master, like jumping and shooting, and goals that test whether the player has mastered them. Many video games also tell a story that adds meaning to the goals, like jumping to rescue a princess or shooting to defend Earth from alien invaders. Game design is the process of creating those challenges and stories.

Video games are designed to require focus and skill.

Game designers create mechanics—systems of abilities, rules, goals, and **feedback** that define how the player interacts with the game. After thinking of fun mechanics, the designer writes a story that fits the challenges of the game and the order in which the player will complete them. Because video games are both stories and challenges, a game designer can begin their work with an idea for either the mechanics or the story.

STEAM Fast Fact:

Nintendo's 1981 arcade game *Donkey Kong* is considered to be the first game to feature jumping over objects as a **mechanic**. It was also one of the first games to have a story shown on the screen, instead of in an instruction manual.

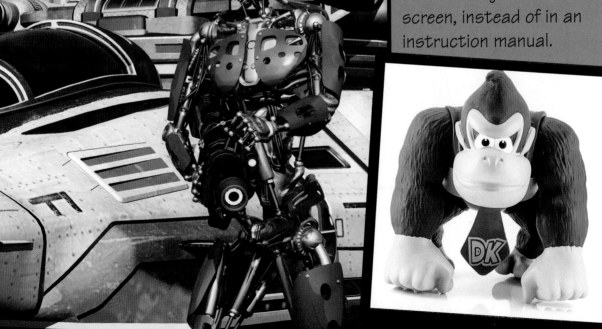

STEAM Spotlight!

Pong was designed by Nolan Bushnell and released in 1972. It was not the first video game ever made, but it was one of the first arcade games. It was simple, based on the rules of tennis, and the instructions printed on the arcade cabinet were just as simple:

1. DEPOSIT QUARTER
2. BALL WILL SERVE AUTOMATICALLY
3. AVOID MISSING BALL FOR HIGH SCORE

Since most people had never played a video game before, it was important to design a game that was easy to explain. Think of your favorite video game. Can you describe the goal of that game in fewer words than the instructions for Pong?

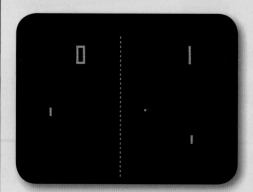

Well-designed games usually have rules and goals that the player can easily see and understand.

A designer must understand the other jobs in the development process to be able to explain their ideas and to work within a specific budget to finish the game on time. Designers also work with game testers to help them understand what the game is supposed to play like when it is finished. Game designers must work well in teams and have at least some skill in all STEAM subjects, particularly art, technology, and mathematics.

Game designers help the development team look at the "big picture" of what the game is supposed to be.

Real STEAM Job: *Ubisoft Game Designer*

Ubisoft is one of the world's leading video game development companies. The company's game designers have worked on many popular games, including the *Rayman, Prince of Persia*, and the *Just Dance* series. A team of Ubisoft game designers creates the story and challenge for a game.

Ubisoft has many popular series, so the designers might already have some ideas. For example, it would be difficult to make a *Just Dance* game without dancing or music! Whether the idea is original or not, the design team must then explain their ideas to the rest of the development team.

Ubisoft representatives demonstrate *Just Dance 4* at a video game expo.

Art and Animation

Artists create the visual elements of video games. Artists draw concept art, images of characters and environments, as a "rough draft" to help the rest of the development team understand what the game should look like. Then, they use advanced computer software to make 3-D models of characters and environments that are used to make the game. Afterward, they draw the images that get placed on top of the 3-D models. These images, called textures, add detail to the virtual world. The finished products are called **art assets**.

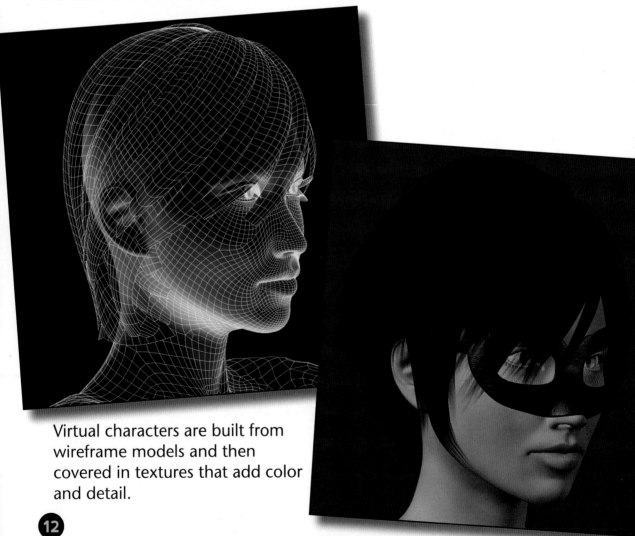

Virtual characters are built from wireframe models and then covered in textures that add color and detail.

Artists create the buildings and characters. Animators add lighting and shadow effects, and make the people and water move realistically.

Animators take the art assets and make them move as if they were actually alive. They make characters walk, jump, and climb in ways that look realistic. They are also responsible for animating the environment. For instance, they make sure that blades of grass will sway in the wind.

Flower, 2009

Both jobs require similar skills, including a strong background in art. Artists and animators are required to have technology skills to draw their images on computers and make 3-D models of characters and environments. They also need to have at least some knowledge in life sciences, especially anatomy, to draw and animate living beings.

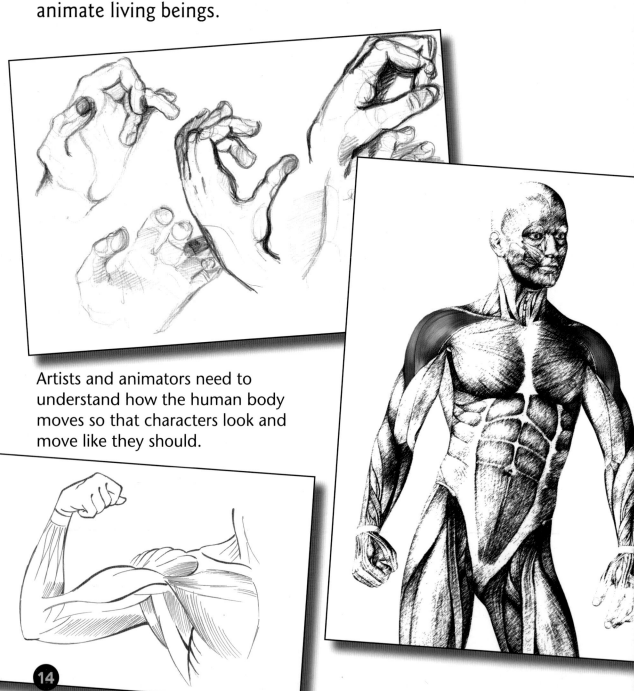

Artists and animators need to understand how the human body moves so that characters look and move like they should.

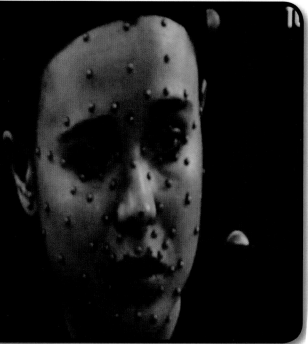

Motion capture, or "Mo Cap," is the process of transposing actors' movements onto in-game characters by recording data from markers placed on their face and body.

STEAM Spotlight!

The video game *L.A. Noire* is a detective game in which players have to decide whether suspects are lying or telling the truth. To create character animations so realistic that players can use their facial expressions as feedback, developer Team Bondi used a brand-new motion capture technique. Instead of using markers to indicate key points on an actor's face, they actually filmed the performance and placed the footage over the 3-D model of the character.

Audio Engineering

If you have ever reached the flagpole at the end of a level in a *Super Mario Bros.* game, then you probably appreciate the importance of sound effects. Players use sound as a type of feedback, a way for the game developers to tell the player, "There is an enemy off screen that you should know about," or in the case of the flagpole, "Hooray for finishing the level!"

Sound is also important for making a game realistic. Just like movies, people really notice when something does not sound correct in a video game—or, even worse, when it does not make any sound at all! Consider the swaying blades of grass from the previous section and imagine if you could not hear them rustle in the wind. Would the virtual environment feel like a real world? Likely, you would probably feel something was wrong.

Sound effects give this player a sense of speed and alert him to other racers closing in from behind.

STEAM in Action!

Try playing your favorite video game with the volume on mute. Is the game easier or more difficult? Think about how the sounds of that game help you perform better or enjoy it more.

Now, think about some of your favorite video game sound effects. What sorts of actions cause the game to make those sounds? Why do you think it was important that the audio engineers made those sound effects so enjoyable?

Audio engineers edit every noise you hear when you play a video game. They make sound effects, record dialogue, and sometimes work with music composers to add a soundtrack. Audio engineers need to have skills in engineering, technology, and math.

Joana Santos works with an audio engineer to give a voice to Jodie Holmes, one of the two player characters in the PlayStation 3 video game *Beyond: Two Souls.*

Programming

Programmers are the core of a game development team. They write computer code in programming languages like C++ that run and control everything in a video game. Programmers code things that we take for granted in the real world, like the laws of physics. Some programmers specialize in coding one specific part of a game, such as **artificial intelligence**, or the behavior of computer-controlled characters.

Real STEAM Job: *Programmer at Epic Games*

Many games require the same basic code, so programmers often create and use advanced software programs called game engines. Most video game developers use game engines because it is more efficient to use a game engine than to write the basic code for every single project.

Epic Games is a development studio that, in addition to making their own games, creates and licenses a game engine for other studios to use. Their Unreal Engine is one of the most popular choices for video game developers.

The action game *Zeno Clash II* was created using Unreal Engine 3.

Programmers need to be independent workers, but also work well as part of a team. They try to create what the game designers want and they need to talk with testers to make sure the video game is coming along well. Often, programmers have to deal with **crunch**, the term development teams use to describe the times when a lot of work needs to be completed before an important deadline.

Programmers usually have a degree in math, computer science, or physics. They must know at least one programming language before getting a job and will usually learn more during their careers. Most employers want to see some samples of code or a game demo, so it is important for students to use their college projects as an opportunity to build a portfolio of work.

When coding the tactical shooter *Nuclear Dawn*, the programmers included multiple resources like maps and menus. Also, unlike most other games, players can even look at the same environment from both first- and third-person perspectives.

The type of environment being depicted in the game, such as this snow-covered factory, can pose different challenges to programmers.

The programmers of this multiplayer game needed to know how to write code to support input from more than one player.

Level Editing

Level editors are hired to build the virtual space in which a video game is played. Some types of video games, like the puzzle game *Tetris*, take place on one screen and do not have characters or a story. However, most modern video games take place in large 3-D environments where players control an avatar, a model of a character that represents the player in the game. Levels can be designed to look like real places, like the city of Venice in *Assassin's Creed II*. Or, they can be designed more like a board game, like the maze in *Pac-Man*. Either way, a level editor must design spaces that are interesting to look at and challenging to navigate.

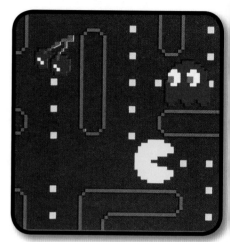

Pac-Man maze

Many modern games feature realistic environments, such as this "Clock Tower" level in *Nuclear Dawn* that depicts realistic Houses of Parliament in a virtual London.

Usually, the layout of a level depends on the mechanics of the game. For example, in a multiplayer game like *Splatoon*, levels are designed to be like sports arenas, but with many different spots that can only be reached by mastering the ability of turning into a squid and swimming through ink. In other games, like the first-person puzzle game *Portal*, the level layout is actually part of the mechanics. In *Portal*, players use a portal gun to shoot two openings of a single portal across a room that is designed to test players' knowledge of gravity, momentum, and other basic concepts in physics.

The level design in *Portal* is an important part of the overall game design. The environments were built to challenge players to learn and master specific actions using the portal gun.

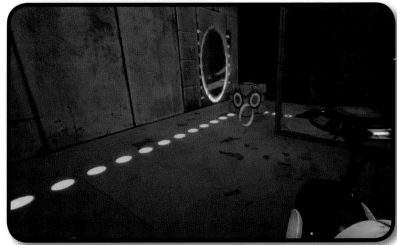

There are several ways that players interested in level editing can develop the skill. Many video games give players tools to make their own levels, such as *Minecraft, LittleBigPlanet,* and *Super Mario Maker.* Also, fans with some knowledge of programming create mods, or modifications, to existing games. Practicing with mods and in-game level editors is a good way to get started, because the programming, art, animation, sound, and mechanics are already in place.

Level editors must have good spatial reasoning skills and should know how to use 3-D modeling programs in order to create complex virtual spaces. They must understand game design theory to work with designers, making sure the levels fit the game's mechanics. They must also know enough programming to work with programmers and artists. Someone who wants to become a level editor can earn a degree in engineering, software development, or design.

QA Testing

Modern video games typically take years to make. They require development teams of dozens, hundreds, or even thousands of people who sometimes work remotely from across the globe. They feature massive open worlds and complex stories, filled with characters that need to act and interact with the player. It is no wonder that video games, like all software, have the potential to malfunction.

Quality assurance (QA) is the process of testing a video game to make sure it works, no matter what the player does to the game. Once a video game is developed to the point of being playable, QA testers are hired to play the game for many hours each day.

A tester's job is to find **bugs**, or mistakes, in video games. Bugs are sometimes the result of bad coding. More often, though, bugs are just part of the job and occur no matter what. When a development team combines so many pieces into one game—characters, environments, player abilities and choices— it is inevitable that there will be problems.

Arno Dorian, the protagonist of *Assassin's Creed: Unity,* missing his face because of a bug that got through testing (left). The bug was patched later in an online update to the game.

STEAM in Action!

Imagine a video game in which the player has to talk to three different non-player characters (NPCs). During each of those three conversations, the player has three dialogue choices. How many possible combinations of choices are there?

$$3^3 = 3 \times 3 \times 3 = 27$$

What if the player has four dialogue choices?

$$3^4 = 3 \times 3 \times 3 \times 3 = 81$$

Now, what if the player can choose the order in which they talk to those NPCs? And, what if the player can make choices that open up or close off different choices at the next conversation?

It is easy to see how complicated a video game can become. In fact, some video games are advertised as having enough combinations of items or interactions that they are basically infinite.

The only way to make sure a video game does not break is by trying to break it. Testers try as many combinations as they can during the development process.

It is the job of a tester to "unmake" the game, to play it in every possible way. This includes walking into walls, jumping into every pit, and talking to characters in the wrong order. Even though they get to play video games, testers do not play games like you would at home. If you have ever ignored a mission prompt in a role-playing game, or started driving backward in a racing game, then you might understand what testing is like.

Testers give the game designers feedback, letting them know how closely the development team has matched the original vision for the game. There are a few correct ways to play a game, but there are many incorrect ways—and testers are tasked with finding them all! Testers must be imaginative and patient in order to find as many bugs as possible. A background in technology and engineering is useful, but not required. Becoming a tester does not require a college degree and is considered a good place to start in the industry.

Methods for Testing

Functionality testing: What you think of when you hear "video game tester?" This involves playing a game to test its fundamental design and to check for programming bugs and glitches.

Compliance testing: Developers license content from other media and they also publish games on consoles made by other companies. These other parties want to know that the game follows all the rules and requirements of any licensing agreements the developer has made.

Compatibility testing: Very important for PC games because players may have different combinations of hardware components and a game needs to run on as many setups as possible.

Localization testing: After translating the text and menus from one region to another, testers will play the localized version of the game to make sure everything is correct.

Soak testing: When testers try to make a game fail by doing all the worst things that players might do while playing at home, including leaving the game paused for hours or clicking the same button hundreds of times.

Beta testing: The first round of testing that is available to the public, meant to crowdsource testing to a much larger group of people and to see how the average player feels about the game.

Regression testing: Once a bug is reported and fixed, testers must check to see if the fix is effective and make sure it does not break something else in the game.

Load testing: Can the game handle as many players as the developers claim? Will it glitch if there are too many characters on-screen at the same time? Testers are required to assess whether the game will continue to function at these full capacities.

Multiplayer testing: Testers play multiplayer modes to test how well the programming can help two copies of the game communicate with each other across an online setup.

Mobile game testing: Testing specifically for mobile games, which often includes all the types of testing listed above.

Community Management

Fans of video games use the Internet to learn about games before they are finished. They also visit websites and forums to share their excitement and learn new strategies. And, since many games have online multiplayer, players form groups (sometimes called "clans") so they can win team matches or complete difficult dungeons together. Players form communities around their favorite video games.

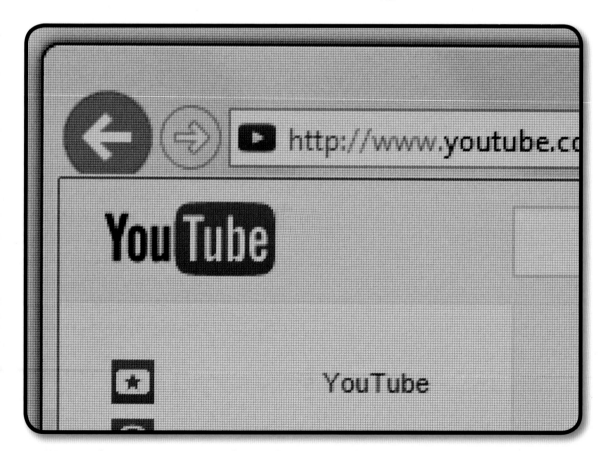

Many players post gameplay videos on websites, such as YouTube and Twitch.

These *World of Warcraft* cosplayers belong to a community of fans that is important to the development studio.

A community manager is someone who helps build a relationship between a game's developers and its community of players. They share news on the game's official website and also patrol the forums to make sure everyone is nice to each other. Community managers speak to the game designers, letting them know what players want from future updates to the game.

It is important for developers and publishers to show their content at video game expos like E3 because fans will read articles and watch videos from the event. High-profile games, such as *Call of Duty: Black Ops II,* tend to be more popular and sell more copies.

ELECTRONIC
ENTERTAINMENT
EXPO

BE THE BATMAN

Often, community managers are the first people to communicate with players when something goes wrong. If a video game is down for maintenance and people start complaining on Internet forums, the community manager responds to the angry comments in a professional manner. A community manager is supposed to keep people happy and excited for a game. They act as a bridge of communication between players and the development team.

Community managers need to know HTML coding so they can update the video game's website. They need to be good writers, too. Many community managers have experience in journalism, advertising, or public relations. While community managers are usually not involved in a game's development, they need to know how it works so they can communicate the process to the public.

HTML is the standard programming language used to create web pages.

```
PE html>
lang='th'>

itle>Wepage Title</title>

meta charset="UTF-8" />
meta name="viewport" content="width=
meta name="description" content="Lor
Fringilla iaculis eros in convallis. A
<meta name="keywords" content="Phasell
<meta name="author" content="Author">

<meta property="og:image" content="http
<meta property="og:url" content="http:/
<meta property="og:title" content="Mund
<meta property="og:description" content=
sollicitudin mollis. Sed sollicitudin te
sollicitudin mollis. Sed sollicitudin
ibero eu sollicitudin mollis. Sed solli
name="geo.position" content="ll.ll
geo.placename" content="Bend
```

Video Game Economics

Video games can have many types of resources, or valuable items, that players can collect, including weapons, gear, and gold. Games like *World of Warcraft* have millions of players collecting, buying, and selling these resources in a **virtual economy**. Development studios hire economists to find a good balance between resources being too easy and too hard to collect.

#FALLOUT4
#BGC2015

Fallout 4

Bethesda's games in the *Fallout* series use bottle caps as a form of currency because in the post-apocalyptic future of the story, they are a rare resource that has become as hard to find as gold.

Economists are people who use math to calculate how much something should cost. They also use facts about how individual people will behave in order to predict how large groups will buy and sell resources. They use this information to estimate prices and advise businesses.

Economists are able to use their knowledge of business and consumer behavior to inform game design.

Video game economists make sure that players do not "break" the virtual economy by finding ways to make resources cheaper or easier to collect. They also help game designers figure out **drop rates**, the probability that rare items will appear after defeating enemies.

STEAM Spotlight!

In the video game *Destiny*, players found an **exploit**, a way of earning more resources faster than the designers intended. In specific spots, players would wait for enemies to appear at a faster rate than anywhere else in the game. More enemies meant more loot, which increased the chance of finding rare items. Eventually, some players spent most of their time in these "loot caves" which increased their resources but made the game less fun. The developer, Bungie, was forced to update the game to remove the exploit.

Loot Cave in *Destiny*

Buy Gold Coins

+5
100
5% more
$0.99

+20
300
20% more
$4.99

+50
800
50% more
$9.99

FREE

Economists help figure out what in-game resources are worth in real money.

Video game economists can also work with real-world money. Free-to-play games are a new type of video game that have **microtransactions**, which is what happens when in-game items cost real money. Economists help the development team decide the **conversion rate**, or how much of the in-game resources the player should receive for spending real money.

Video game economists need a strong background in math to run the complex calculations for figuring out prices. They also need to understand the technology of video games, so they can collect the information to make those calculations. This is a new job in the video game industry but, with the rise in popularity of free-to-play games, there is a great demand for economists.

STEAM Job Facts

Game Designer

Important Skills: art, writing, storytelling, programming, leadership, systems analysis, judgement and decision making

Important Knowledge: game design theory, English, computers

College Major: game design, creative writing, computer design

Artist / Animator

Important Skills: art, software editing, programming, storytelling

Important Knowledge: computer science, anatomy and architecture, animation, filmmaking

College Major: fine art, graphic design, illustration

Audio Engineer

Important Skills: music composition and performance, computer science, software editing, creative thinking

Important Knowledge: science, engineering and technology, design, mechanics, mathematics, electronics

College Major: sound/audio engineering, music recording, computer science

Programmer

Important Skills: computer science, mathematics, complex problem-solving, systems analysis

Important Knowledge: computers, programming, engineering, design

College Major: mathematics, physics, computer science

Level Editor

Important Skills: spatial reasoning, art, creative design

Important Knowledge: architecture, computers, design, game design theory, information technology, programming

College Major: design, software development, engineering

QA Tester

Important Skills: systems analysis, patience and persistence, communication

Important Knowledge: game industry awareness, game design theory, English, writing, programming, information technology

College Major: English, communication, computer science, design

Community Manager

Important Skills: writing, communication, computer science, art

Important Knowledge: communication, public relations, web design, game design

College Major: journalism, advertising, public relations, communication

Economist

Important Skills: systems analysis, complex problem-solving, judgement and decision making

Important Knowledge: economic game theory, mathematics, computer science

College Major: economics, mathematics

Glossary

art assets (ahrt AS-ets): any finished 3D model, sound effect, or other piece of art that is used in making a video game

artificial intelligence (ahr-tuh-FISH-uhl in-TEL-i-juhns): the ability of computer-controlled characters to act with intent and react to other characters, including the player

bugs (bughs): mistakes in development, either in coding or design, that usually result from the complexity of combining multiple systems

conversion rate (kuhn-VUR-zhuhn rayt): the amount of in-game resources the player receives for spending real money; similar to exchange rates of real-world currency between countries

crunch (kruhnch): the point in a development cycle when the team works overtime to reach important deadlines

drop rates (drahp raytz): the ratio of common, uncommon, and rare items that appear after completing challenges in a video game, usually from defeating enemies

exploit (EK-sploit): taking advantage of bugs to perform actions in ways the designers did not intend; used as a way to bypass challenges and reach goals more quickly

feedback (FEED-bak): any signal sent by a game to the player to indicate some change in the game status, usually caused by the player's input

mechanic (muh-KAN-ik): a system of abilities, rules, goals, and feedback that defines how the player interacts with the game

microtransactions (MYE-kroh-tran-SAK-shuhns): when players pay real-world money for in-game items; most common in mobile "free-to-play" games

virtual economy (VUR-choo-uhl i-KAH-nuh-mee): the exchange of virtual resources inside a video game between the environment, players, and non-player characters

Index

Show What You Know

1. What does STEAM stand for?
2. What STEAM skills are used in game development?
3. Which job is a good place to start working in game development?
4. What type of background does a community manager usually have?
5. In what two ways can an economist help with video game development?

Websites to Visit

www.code.org

www.gamestarmechanic.com

www.kodugamelab.com

About The Author

Kenneth Rosenberg is a communication scholar who studies the psychological effects of media, particularly the ways that people use video games to interact with stories about ethics and morality. He is a fan of everything Nintendo and likes to host *Rock Band* parties.

Meet The Author!
www.meetREMauthors.com

PHOTO CREDITS: Cover: Android in fire © Mike H, female head © dimitris_k, female soldier © Mike H; pages 4-5 game screen shot © Mike H, audio engineer © Peter Mayer Fotos, programmer © Dean Drobot; pages 6-7 background © Mike H, guy playing video game © jcjgphotography, Donkey Kong © Nicescene; pages 8-9 Pong game © Chris Rand, meeting © Rawpixel.com; Page 10-11: Just Dance game shot © Barone Firenze; pages 12-13 © wireframes © design36, finished female head © dimitrus_k, stone arches image © Mike H; Pages 14-15 hand sketches © Ralwel, arm muscle © Dolly, chest anatomy © design36,Page 15 Mo Cap © G0r3cki | Dreamstime.com, Minecraft Game on phone © denizen; pages 16-17 © Blackregis; page 18 © lipid, page 19 © G0r3cki | Dreamstime.com; Page 20 © Arne9001 | Dreamstime.com, page 21 screenshots © ACE TEAM; pages 22-24 © Nuclear Dawn by InterWave Studios – http://www.interwavestudios.com; pages 27 © John Williams RUS; Page 28 Arno with intact face © Barone Firenze; Page 30 © Dejan Stanic Micko; page 32 © dips, page 33 © Elvis untot/Wikimedia; pages 34-35 Electronics expo entrance © logbook, x-box and Playstation pics © Barone Firenze, kids playing game © Dikiiy; pages 36-37 html code close-up © inspiration; pages 38-38 Fallout Wasteland © https://www.flickr.com/photos/97049488@N05/8969592430/ Vault boy © Tim Bartel, Flickr https://creativecommons.org/licenses/by-sa/2.0/; page 40 © Ditty_about_summer, page 41 expo shot © Lauren Elisabeth; page 42 © Ico Maker. Images on following pages are from Shutterstock.com: All cover images, pages 4-7, pages 9-18 except *Flower* screenshot page 13, *Pacman* maze page 24, page 27, 30, 32, 34-36, 40-42

Edited by: Keli Sipperley

Cover and Interior design by: Nicola Stratford   www.nicolastratford.com

Library of Congress PCN Data

STEAM Jobs in Game Development / Kenneth Rosenberg
(STEAM Jobs You'll Love)
ISBN 978-1-68191-741-2 (hard cover)
ISBN 978-1-68191-842-6 (soft cover)
ISBN 978-1-68191-934-8 (e-Book)
Library of Congress Control Number:2016932704

Printed in the United States of America, North Mankato, Minnesota

Also Available as: